Hot Small Business Ideas!

25 Smokin' Hot Start Up Business Ideas To Spark Your Entrepreneurship Creativity And Have You In Business Fast!

I0503168

James Harper

Copyright © 2013 James Harper

STOP!!! Before you read any further....Would you like to know the Success Secrets of how to make Passive Income Online?

If your answer is yes, then you are not alone. Thousands of people are looking for the secret to learning how to create their own online passive income style business.

If you have been searching for these answers without much luck, you are in the right place!

Because I want to make sure to give you as much value as possible for purchasing this book, right now for a limited time you can get 3 incredible bonuses for free.

At the end of this book I describe all 3 bonuses. You can access them at the end. But for those of you that want to grab your bonuses right now. See below.

Just Go Here For Free Instant Access:

www.OperationAwesomeLife.com/FreeBonuses

Legal Notice

Disclaimer Notice

Table Of Contents

Introduction

I want to thank you and congratulate you for purchasing the book, *"Hot Small Business Ideas!: 25 Smokin' Hot Start Up Business Ideas To Spark Your Entrepreneurship Creativity And Have You In Business Fast!"*.

This book contains 25 proven small business ideas to find the right niche for you to become successful.

Congratulations on making the first step towards a better life for yourself and your loved ones. Creating a business is the financially smartest thing you can do in today's often volatile job market. As more and more folks get laid off in the rapidly changing economy we live in, more and more people are looking for a more stable source of income in which they have better control of.

I could go on and on about the benefits of owning and operating your own business, but I won't because that's not why you are here. You already know you want to own your own business and make your own decisions; you just need to know where to channel your drive and hard work. In this book you will find 25 of the Hottest Small Business Ideas for today!

One thing I have learned over the years of being an entrepreneur is that if you don't have passion for the business you are in - then you most likely will not make it. I'm here to fuel that passion by giving you some great ideas you can really sink your teeth into.

Thanks again for purchasing this book, I hope you enjoy it!

Chapter 1 - Starting Your Own Online Business

Nobody gets rich by remaining an employee forever. You need to take greater risks, invest and be your own boss to earn more and provide a much better life for yourself and your family. That is practically how your bosses does it.

There is no better time to start a small business than now. Marketing has never been easier, thanks to the multitude of channels, tools and online facilities that help you have success in marketing without spending a dime. The awareness in business management is also higher, so you will have more time and opportunities to thrive in your chosen industry and make a name for yourself.

Starting your own business is not just about the extra income; it is about the extra time for yourself and your family, and all the comfortable and luxurious perks that come with it. Starting your own smoking hot business is your ultimate ticket to better living, having all resources to buy whatever you want and plan ahead without having to consider vacation/leave credits, office schedules and unrelenting superiors.

Being your own boss is a life-changing decision that can steer your whole life – upwards if you have the dedication and willingness to learn and develop your craft, or downwards if you cannot commit to your decision.

For a starter, you will be introduced to the hottest online businesses you can possibly start.

1. Amazon Affiliate

Affiliate programs are smoking hot; double that for Amazon. This is the new version of product consignment, only done online. You will need to do the marketing, promotions and reviews preferably in the form of blogging to get more customers for Amazon's listed products. This is a fulltime online business with unlimited earning opportunities.

Pros:

- *Famous* – Amazon is the top online shopping site all around the world. The name sells in itself. The program is reliable and has been around for more than a decade now. It is definitely the most trusted affiliate program today.

- *Flexible time* – All the marketing efforts and website setups are all in your good time. You can keep earning while sleeping, so management is not stressful.

- *Low-cost* – Your only expense is the domain and server, although there are free providers you can choose from.

Cons:

- *Might take time to pick up* – Gaining huge online traffic and website contents may take time, perhaps months before you can actually earn. The good thing is that when it picks up, there is no stopping it.

- *Requires intense internet marketing know-how* – Millions of people all around the world do marketing online. If you want to standout, you need to master the techniques and learn continuously.

2. Niche Blogging

Blogging doesn't run out of steam, and it continues to be the new newspaper, magazine, paperback, diary and variety show. According to Yahoo, the blogging industry recorded its highest revenue in 2013, and there is no sign of backing down anytime soon. Average niche bloggers earn anywhere from $1,000 to $15,000 a month, the latter implying the full-timers.

Pros:

- *Unlimited source of income* – You can earn from ad vendors, paid advertising, PPC, paid publicity and promotions, affiliate programs and dozens more of innovative online opportunities.

- *Easy to set up* – You only need to have flair in writing – informing and entertaining at the same time. Setting up your blog is easy and in fact, you can have it for free. Just pick a topic and niche market you want to tap, and be the best in it.

Cons:

- *Traffic problems* – Online traffic can be a big problem if you will only focus on the actual blogging part. Remember that this is a business; thus, it involves intense marketing and customer relations.

- *Requires patience* – You can't write and have thousands of readers right away. Even the most successful bloggers today needed to build their fan-base over time.

3. SEO Firm

SEO (search engine optimization) is the life of websites, both non-profit and commercial. SEO dictates the competition. It doesn't run out of market. Your business' goal here is to get clients on top of search engines and get them the traffic and conversion that they are targeting. If you have advance knowledge in web and graphic designing, SEO writing, SEM (search engine marketing) and internet marketing strategies, you are ready to get some clients and build websites for them. A team of five specialists is already enough to handle a pool of business websites.

Pros:

- *Easy to set up* – What you do when you make your own website or blog is the same thing you will do for your clients. You might just need support staff for the other technical aspects and to finish projects on deadlines.

- *Low-cost* – Most likely, you already have a usable computer. You only need to buy different software (you can get them for free if you are adept in online sourcing) and additional computers – perhaps rent a server.

- *Easy to market* – Your body of work speaks for itself. The market is unlimited, and your efficiency in the job will dictate how far you can get in the industry.

Cons:

- *Tough competition* – At the end of the day, your client's online success (in terms of traffic generation, search engine ranking, etc.) will gauge your reputation. There is only one page to aim at but, there are thousands of websites competing. The competition is not only between you and other SEO firms. You need to remember that your client's stand in the competition is also your responsibility.

4. Graphic Designing

You can launch this business as a part of SEO services for company websites and professional bloggers. However, a graphic designing company can also stand alone as it really was before SEO became the buzz. If you are adept in designing, working on your own shouldn't be a problem at all.

You can cater to bloggers and social media addicts who want to take their accounts to another level (many Facebook-ers and Youtube-ers hire graphic and video designers and editors to professionalize their accounts). You can also cater to special occasions, such as weddings, birthday parties, launchings, etc.

Pros:

- *Wide, unlimited market* – Graphic designing services have been here even before they were integrated with SEO. Specifically, those who hire graphic

- designers belong to small-scale businesses and private individuals. Your own talent will be your own setback.

- *Low startup cost* – You need a piece of computer, internet connection, printer and a whole lot of creative ingenuity. Depending on the volume of your clientele, you can expand in resources as you expand in operation.

Cons:

- *Professionally limiting* – Many experts believe that graphic designing should just be the beginning of a more expansive business because this alone is very limiting, professional at least. There's not exactly a next level, unless you include other services and provide tangible products as well, such as selling your own souvenir items or expanding to other SEO services as well.

5. eBook Self-Publication

Book and eBook writing are both professions, but self-publication of eBooks is a business. It involves end-to-end processes, from the writing to editing, cover designing to online publication, and marketing to selling. Many bloggers have already shifted to fulltime eBook self-publication as the potential income is higher.

Amazon and Barnes and Noble are the two top online destinations when it comes to eBook publication. You will likely receive just a percentage of the eBook price, but the accumulated earnings are enough to top your monthly income from a fulltime office job. Selling through your own website is also a lucrative idea, but only if you attract huge online traffic and has already set yourself as one of the leaders in your niche industry.

Pros:

- *Unlimited earning potential* – As of 2012, eBook sales have already surpassed hardcover sales, but only next to paperback sales. In the next five to 10 years, it is expected that online publication will be the most marketable form of publication.

- *A potential launch pad to stardom* – This business is not only about the money – millions of money. It is also about legacy, name and popularity.

- *Easy to execute* – Writing shouldn't be a problem. Most of your efforts will go to the cover design and marketing strategies.

Cons:

- *Needs decent online presence* – If you will market your own eBooks, you need to have an existing market-base. Otherwise, starting from scratch will take time to convert into sales.

- *Possible failure* – The failure in the self-publication industry is really high. Many eBook writers don't even crack the 200-sales threshold. If you think your writing skills and creativity are not enough to make a name for yourself, better choose another business.

6. eBay Trading

eBay is the best channel to start a trading business because all types of products are allowed, both new and used. The site is famous for its cheap finds, so pulling a chunk of the market should not be a problem.

You can source out your products from wholesalers, abroad, garage sales, or you can restore old items to make them new.

Pros:

- *High traffic volume* – Six out of 10 internet users have bought an item from eBay. That is how often eBay makes a sales, which means that market is far from being saturated anytime soon.

- *Easy to set up* – When you already have products to sell, you only need a camera, computer and basic knowledge in setting up an eBay account. You can do your own internet marketing, but eBay is already an established shopping destination. Customers go to the site without prodding.

- *Low startup cost* – Depending on your items, your capital can be as low as a couple of hundreds of dollars. It doesn't matter if you sell second-hand items.

Cons:

- *Difficulty with logistics* – This shouldn't really be a problem because dealing with forwarding and logistic company, both local and international, is now simpler. Nonetheless, you need to take care of it as well, which means extra work.

7. Content Creating

Others call it SEO and technical writing, but content writing is more than just a single component of a fulltime SEO firm. Content writing is less focused on internet marketing stuff – just plain quality content. In the 90s, content writing referred to the outsourced company magazine contents, that included internal newsletters, free magazine giveaways (as a part of store promos) and local ads.

Today, content writing primarily refers to website and blog writing, mostly of private organizations that use their websites not as primary marketing channels but as information centers (which is true for most consumer products that do not really sell online).

Pros:

- *High expected revenue* – Yahoo considers content writing as one of the biggest profession for the next 50 years, especially now that everything is shifting to online publication. The revenue and market are likely to expand without stopping.

- *Simple organizational structure* – A small content writing business doesn't even need to have an office. Most similar companies pool writers online and have them work in virtual offices. You can even do it by yourself if you will take one client at a time.

Cons:

- *Quality concerns* – For a bigger clientele, quality control might be a problem, especially when you do not have in-house editors to help you do quality control, proofreading and copyediting.

8. Server Management

Buying a dedicated server is not something that many small businesses can afford or are even willing to invest in. Server management companies then buy a server space and have it leased out to small companies. You can also have your own server and have it rented as shared server to several clients.

In addition, you must offer support and website management services.

Pros:

- *Huge ROI* – Leasing out a server alone may not incur impressive income, but because of the additional services, you can place a huge premium on top.

- *Huge market-base* – This is a very timely business, so relevant in today's business environment that will not run out of prospective clients in the next few years.

Cons:

- *Requires technical expertise* – Basic knowledge in server management is not enough. You need to have advance skills to make sure that your services are on top.

- *Limited clients* – The size of your clientele will depend on the size of your server.

Chapter 2 - Starting Your Business In The Food Industry

9. Concept Diner

A diner can operate in as simple as a mom-and-pop setup. With a really good menu, not to mention someone to cook it, you can already open your own hole-in-the-wall diner. However, the trend today in the food industry is concept dining, a term that veers away from its traditional meaning of serving specific types of cuisines, such as American, Mexican, Asian and others.

Concept dining has evolved in a way that it now involves intricate and very exact store concepts to provide not only a different ambience but a whole new presentation. Sports bars, food trucks and Hooters are the most prominent concept diners you can find.

Concept dining covers food packaging and serving, store setup, staffs and practically anything that can make it standout from the rest. If you have enough money to spend, food trucks are the best option.

Pros:

- *Fast ROI* – A concept diner has an average ROI time of six to 12 months. Compared to other store-operating businesses, that time is certainly impressive.

- *Recession-proof* – The food industry is recession-proof, so you are likely to thrive even during economic hardships.

- *Stationary operation* – The customers come to you, so your concentration is in the diner and food development alone. Many families prefer this kind of business because everybody meets in one place, literally and figuratively.

Cons:

- *Requires intensive food knowledge* – You shouldn't only have a wide knowledge in restaurant setups or food tasting;

you should also be excellent in cooking. You can hire a chef (which is the usual thing to do), but better chefs tend to be more expensive.

- *More requirements* – Because it involves health, security and safety of the public, expect that the business requirements will also be a lot stricter.

- *Has expected lifespan* – Diners are generally given three to seven years to operate and earn. After that, it might wane down. Extension will depend on the management's capacity to innovate strategies and develop their menu.

10. Personal Chef

The market has never been this large for personal chefs. A few years back, clients were limited to millionaires who need extra hands in the kitchen during parties and large gatherings. Today, personal chefs are also being contracted by families who do not really have time to shop, cook and serve meals, especially during important occasions such as birthdays, get-togethers, reunions and family days,

You can be your own team, can be a mom-and-pop business or hire just another chef or two to assist you when dealing with clients.

Pros:

- *Fast ROI* – Most of the time, you only need to invest on basic kitchen necessities that you like to use on your own, such as knives and pans (most materials will come from the client). Your main investment is free – your cooking expertise and your palate.

- *Huge revenue* – Chefs are some of the highest paid professionals. Theirs are skills that cannot be learned alone in culinary schools.

Cons:

- *Requires personal expertise in cooking* – Hiring a chef to do most of the work is not advisable because sooner or later, your chef will be on his/her own, leaving you with nothing. After all, your chef has the skills while you only have the contacts (which can be earned easily).

- *Very critical job* – It involves health and sanitation, which means that your accountability is higher. Clients who are willing to spend for such service are also very good food critiques, placing you on the chopping block every single day.

Chapter 3 - Starting Your Business In The Beauty And Fitness Industry

11. Dance Studio

Thanks to famous TV programs such as So You Think You Can Dance, Dancing with the Stars, ABDC and Glee, not to mention the myriad of dance movies and musicals in cinemas, the demand for dance studios have peaked in the past three years. The influence of pop culture is definitely sinking in to the public's consciousness that dancing is now part of being "hip" and "cool."

Pros:

- *Doesn't require a dancer for an owner* – You can build a dance studio, provide complete equipment and not be a dancer at all. Dance lessons and choreography services are definitely big advantages, but the studio alone is a lucrative business in itself.

- *Easy management* – You can be your own management team and just hire one or two staffs to help you clean up every closing.

- *Easy setup* – Once the studio is complete, there's nothing much to do but market and manage. Your store is your own commodity.

Cons:

- *Takes long to recover investment* – Although a stable business, the time it takes to recover your initial investment is not impressively fast.

12. Nail Salon

Thanks to reality TV shows and stars, nails are now receiving the same attention as hairs have. The vainer women get, the better for this business. Even high-fashion magazines have already picked up nail art as a form of exquisite beauty.

Although this business primarily caters to women customers, rest assured that this niche market is enough to keep it thriving in the years to come.

Pros:

- *Flexible market class* – You can serve high-end market or offer high-end services for low prices. The best thing about nail care and nail art is that they don't have to be expensive all the time, yet you can always add a premium for your services.

- *Ticket to popularity* – You can be a successful trader but not become a household name, but when you make a name in the beauty and fashion industry, fame follows. And that is all you need to climb the top of the industry.

Cons:

- *High capital* – Nail salons are considered niche beauty businesses. That means, most likely than not, you will attract the high-end market more. That entails investing on sophisticated store layouts and equipment, high-end nail care products and multiple store personnel.

13. Fitness Training

Fortunately, Americans are now becoming health and fitness conscious. The rise to popularity of Zumba, Butt Lift and other fitness programs is a strong proof of that. Many people fail to meet success by working out on their own; thus, fitness trainers become in demand.

Pros:

- *Unlimited clientele* – You can have as much clients as you want as your time permits. But even with limited time, there are ways to handle multiple clients at a time.

- *Easy management* – You can be your own team or partner with fitness gyms. The management only involves managing your program, your time and your clients.

Cons:

- *Requires certifications and other credentials* – You cannot start this business if you are not a certified fitness trainer. You may also need to get separate program-specific certifications from the program creators.

Chapter 4 - Starting Your Business In The Trading Industry

14. Antique Shop

As technology continues to evolve and furniture items adapt more modern designs and functionalities, antiques are more valued and tagged as collectibles. Always keep in mind that time appraises monetary value and importance. In this generation of remote-controlled recliners and fiber optic wall racks, wooden antiques become more precious and coveted.

Pros:

- *Easy to sell* – Rare items sell on their own. Antique collectors are very concentrated market segments. Usually, people who buy antiques belong to the upper market class.

- *Easy to set* up – You need a store, products and customers. The set-up is very basic. No product development is needed.

Cons:

- *Harder to find* – Looking for worthy antiques to sell is not an easy task. You need to scour deeply all possible sources, from private homes to the black market. Looking for items abroad with significant cultural value is also the best solution.

- *Requires expertise in antiquing* – You need to have the "eye" for antiques, including history of sources, nature of materials, delicate caring and pricing. You need to master the classification of antiques and vintage items (there's a thin line between the two).

15. Golf Store

Golf will not beat American football as the most popular sports in the U.S. anytime soon, but its potential in the supplies market is really huge. Tiger Woods might have tainted golf a bit, but many celebrities are now showing interest in the sports. And you should bank on it too.

This business can sell golf supplies (e.g. balls, clubs, bags, carts), golf apparels (e.g. shoes, shirts, caps, short pants), golf-related gadgets and golf lessons.

Pros:

- *Huge potential* – Amazon has recorded its highest sales on golf products last year, and according to PGA America, the sports has generated 10% increase in activity, which means more people are now paying attention to the sports. Women alone have spent millions of dollars on clubs last year.
- *Caters to niche market* – Your market is very concentrated. That makes marketing and customer relations management much easier.

Cons:

- *Location specific* – A store will not sell well if the location is not well chosen. You need to find a location with good concentration or traffic of golf enthusiasts, and possibly, close to golf clubs.

16. Product Consignee

Many businesses have products to sell but do not have the capacity to store, distribute and retail. This is where you enter the picture. Getting a contract for consignment is really simple, provided that you can present a sound and structured plan of consignment. This covers arranging the logistical and storage requirements, distribution, reselling and inventory.

In this generation, businesses are fond of taking shortcuts with their processes, outsourcing included. You will tap into that need and get your share in the service-oriented industry.

Pros:

- *High profit margin* – Because products will come in volumes, your projected profit margin is really impressive, compared to other types of trading businesses.

- *High success rate* – Consignment is a business model with really high success rate.

Cons:

- *Time-consuming* – If you are looking forward to owning your own home business, this is not the one for you. This needs a lot of commitment and time to work out. You need to be hands on with everything, from the time you receive the consignment down to their disposal.

- *High capital requirement* – Usually, a line of credit will be given to consignees. However, this will not suffice if you penetrate a wider market circulation. Added to this are the initial contracts with the logistics and forwarding companies, warehousing requirements, personnel (you will have lots of it) and retailing.

17. Soap and Perfume Making

The transition from chemical to natural components is still going on when it comes to toiletries, soap and perfume making. Even the essential oil business has never been this big. With proper use of internet marketing and online selling, you can make this business big.

Enroll on several soap and perfume making seminars and have your skills develop as you experiment on different scents and concoctions. You also need to create attractive packaging to make it a success.

Pros:

- *Fast ROI* – You earn as you sell. The return on income is really fast compared to trading bigger, more expensive items.

- *High profit margin* – Average profit is 250% a piece. You cannot have that kind of margin in a food business.

- *Flexible time* – You produce and market your products on your own good time.

- *Perennial business* – It is both seasonal and perennial. A really good way to earn money all-year round.

Cons:

- *Requires training and product development period* – The time you need before you can go fulltime on your business may take months. This includes all the training and development period for you to come up with sales-worthy products.

Chapter 5- Starting Your Own Service-Oriented Business

18. Digital Security

This business can start small by catering to residential properties and small businesses. It covers 24/7 surveillance, digital and actual monitoring, security device supplementation and installation, and risk assessment. You can start with five to 10 people, or hire just two staffs if you will only supply security devices to private homes. The devices are not limited to cameras, but to alarm systems and digital recorders as well.

Pros:

- *Timely* – Digital security has never been this in-demand, and the market is expected to continue growing.

- *Wide market* – You will never run out of market. In fact, there is no need to tap a niche market because every property, private and commercial, now use digital security.

- *Fast ROI (return on income)* – You earn as you sell. With added risk assessment and installation services, you can already double the price and earn 200%.

Cons:

- *Requires technical ability* – Supplying and installing digital security devices are not something that can be learned overnight or merely through online research. You need actual training and certification from industry-recognized organizations.

- *Potentially high capital* – Digital security devices are potentially expensive. You may need to shell out as much as $25,000 for it. Nonetheless, a $5,000 capital will still do well especially if you will focus on risk assessment and surveillance services.

19. Business Consultancy

If you are well-versed in a particular field, you can either open your business in that industry or help others open and operate their businesses in that industry. With the advent of online businesses, more and more people like you are trying to crack the small-to-medium industry and make a name for themselves. Consultants like you will guide them to the top and become a figure of your own in the industry.

Your premium (service fee) will initially depend on your experience, achievements, connections and education. From there, the success of your clients will determine how much you can price your service.

Pros:

- *Easy marketing* – Having businesses for your clients work as marketing on its own. When you penetrate a circle of businesses, your performance becomes your advertisement. Usually, word-of-mouth suffices.

- *Easy setup and management* – There's nothing really to manage here but yourself and your time.

- *Huge income* – Experts get the biggest chunk of service-oriented revenues. In a sense, consultants are the lifelines of businesses, that's why they are expensive.

Cons:

- *Demands high level of expertise* – One out of 20 people has the characteristics of a good businessman. One of 20 businessmen has the ability to standout and become a consultant for other businesses. You need to understand the industry more than the actual businessmen, so the demand in expertise is incredibly high.

- *Needs extensive network connections* – Oftentimes, consultants also provide industry connections. Many businessmen take years to have that kind of information, something that you should readily have.

20. *Events Management*

This industry is rapidly growing every year as more events are staged and people are becoming too demanding when it comes to conceptualization, execution and management. Simple events that do not require extensive preparations a few decades ago are now celebrated on a different scale. Even dogs now have their own fashion shows and concept parties are the trend.

If you love organizing things, have the flare in creating memorable concepts, can work as a team player, and most importantly, have all the connections of other service-providers related to events management, this is absolutely the small business for you.

The best thing about this is that you can work on your own and just have the other aspects of the events contracted to other businesses (e.g. catering, sounds and lights, security, etc.).

Pros:

- *Low startup cost* – Many event organizers start with nothing but their creativity, management skills, people skills and contacts. From there, you can expand your sources as more clients come in.

- *Huge market potential* – With events management, you can create your own market rather than tap already existing markets. That is basically how events management grew to what it is today.

- *Flexible* – Although at first, the demand may not be that much for you to work five days a week, the revenue is still enough to top an office worker's paycheck. This is while your time remains flexible.

Cons:

- *Pays higher for niche markets* – This is both good and bad. An event organizer who caters to a niche market receives higher professional fee. The downside of focusing on only one market is that you might run out of clients at some point.

- *Possibly seasonal* – Some niche markets are seasonal, so you need to choose your market wisely and have a back-up plan.

21. HR Consulting Firm

As more small businesses start to transform their homes and computers into virtual offices, fewer resources are placed on essential business departments and facilities, such as human resources. As an HR consulting firm, your job is to provide talents and employees to other companies that do not have time and facilities to do the screening and hiring themselves.

This business is in charge from end to end HR processes, from the collection and selection of applicants, down to the screening and hiring.

Pros:

- *Huge market-base* – The trend in small business setups is minimizing facilities and personnel while maximizing outsourcing possibilities. You have a huge market ahead of you.

- *Minimal startup resources* – All you need are experience in human resources and management, connections and a small office. You will greatly rely on your skills for this, so material resources are at their minimum.

Cons:

- *Requires an office* – Unfortunately, you cannot open an HR consultation firm without your own office because people will be coming to you, both clients and applicants. Even if you purely screen online, you should still have an actual office.

- *Requires extensive HR experience* – You cannot bank on your capital here. You need a real investment in experience and expertise, which takes years to achieve.

22. Home Health Care

America's graying population need a lot of attention and caring. Fortunately, many families now refuse to place their elders in nursing homes and just have them attended at homes instead.

You can transform your home to a health care facility or offer on-call services.

Pros:

- *Growing market* – According to Franchise Business Review, home health care franchises are the third largest franchise business in the U.S. today. That means more nursing facilities and health care companies are expanding to tap the growing demand for health services at home.

- *High profit return* – Believe it or not, home health care businesses have the highest profit return than any form of franchise business.

- *Continuous expansion opportunities* – It is estimated that such services will continue to grow through 2050, chiefly due to the country's graying population.

Cons:

- *Stricter business requirements* – Unlike trading business, home health care business comes with more legal requirements that cover health and sanitation permits, professional certifications, business permits and a whole lot more.

- *Requires a licensed health care professional* – It is either you are a licensed health care professional, or you will hire licensed people. The ideal ratio is one professional for five to 10 patients. If you need to resort to hiring, your investment will be much higher.

23. Home Restoration Services

Many American families now prefer home restoration over house reconstructions because the former is cheaper and more practical. After the recession, many people realized how important saving on home improvements and maintenance is rather than spending on unnecessary home reconstructions.

Actually, even "home restoration" is a broad term that mostly refers to post-calamity restoration services and home improvement services.

Pros:

- *High profit returns* – The ROI is not as fast as in other industries, but the profit return is incredibly impressive.

- *Wide market-base* – Unless you will transform this business into a niche company (i.e. catering solely on roofing or flooring services), your market will remain really wide.

Cons:

- *High initial investment* – That includes industrial-size equipment, vehicles and manpower.

- *Requires advance expertise* – You need to be a professional with years of experience in this field to make it work.

24. *Garage Sale Management*

With the volatility of the real estate industry, many people resort to garage sales to dispose possessions. Garage sales have surged into popularity in the last two years alone, thanks to reality shows that show how much value can be earned just by disposing extra trinkets and hoarded possessions.

You can contract home association to let you manage garage sales for all members, or you can buy expiring storage contracts and sell whatever things you can get from them.

Pros:

- *Impressive profit margin* – You can earn up to 1,000%. That explains everything.

- *Easy sourcing* – Compared to sourcing for trading products, getting items for garage sales is much easier and cheaper.

- *Fast ROI* – You can recover your initial capital right at the first successful sale.

Cons:

- *Might require travelling* – You cannot focus on just one location if you want your business to continue flourishing.

25. Cleaning Services

Cleaning companies have grown in number by 50% in the last five years. As companies realize how much they can save by taking out in-house cleaning and maintenance services, cleaning services also thrive and get a big chunk of companies' budgets. Now, even residential cleaning is becoming more popular as it retains privacy without sacrificing domestic cleanliness.

Pros:

- *Growing market* – The market continues to expand, so you will have many more years to earn.

- *Long-term contracts* – The profit margin is not really that big, but with long-term contracts, your source of income will be much stable – not supremely huge, but guaranteed.

Cons:

- *Requires huge initial investment* – You have to invest on training, equipment, vehicle, office, warehouse and personnel. It might take more than a year (or years) before you can fully recover your capital, but at least you are guaranteed with income for the next years to come.

Conclusion

Thank you again for purchasing this book!

I hope this book was able to help you to find the perfect niche in the small business arena.

But unfortunately, you can't just expect to read this book and be a professional business man. It takes practice to become great at anything in life, and being a great businessman is no different. So get out there and begin this journey, and don't forget to have fun along the way and not take yourself too seriously!

If you know of anyone else that could benefit from the information presented here please inform them of this book.

The next step is to get started fulfilling your dreams and never look back!

Finally, if you enjoyed this book, please take the time to share your thoughts and post a review on Amazon. It'd be greatly appreciated!

Thank you and good luck!

Preview Of:

How To Be Rich

Discover How To Be Rich Using Money Rules Of The Rich To Make Money, Gain Passive Income, Be Debt Free, And Financially Free In 6 Simple Steps!

Introduction

I want to thank you and congratulate you for purchasing the book, "Money Rules Of The Rich - 6 Simple Steps To Wealth Creation".

This book contains proven steps and strategies on how to think and operate your financial affairs like the wealthy.

Have you ever wondered how you can take two people working the same job with the same salary and one seems to always have money while the other seems to always be broke? Or have you ever wondered how a self made millionaire is able to rise out of the lower level of society while another seems to be trapped?

Well, if you have ever contemplated on these things, then you are in the right place! There is a process to wealth creation, some may call it a formula, but it is undoubtedly not the result of luck. If you want to get from A-Z, if you want to get to the top of the mountain, you have to have a roadmap. This is your roadmap.

Sometimes the hardest thing to do is to start! Unfortunately this is also the most important part. If you never start, you will never accomplish anything in life, let alone major ambitions. Please don't delay any longer! Stop putting your future on hold, and begin at once towards the amazing life you were born to live and should already be enjoying! I wish you the best of luck in this endeavor, and hope you will choose this book and its principles to be a part of your exciting accent to the top!

Thanks again for purchasing this book, I hope you enjoy it!

Chapter 1 - Living Within 80% Or Less Of Your Income

The fact that you have an income doesn't mean that you need to spend all those income as you please. Sure you can – but you should not if you want to become rich. Many people believe that they work to live and vice versa, thus making them slaves of the vicious cycle of "working for a living". This need not happen to you, and it certainly would not if you follow the rules on accumulating wealth.

The first thing that you need to remember is that you should live within 80% or less of your income. Yes, you heard it right! You cannot go all out with your pay check if you want to become rich. The next question would be: what would you do with your money?

As a basic rule, you need some part of your income to be able to afford your basic needs, i.e. water, food, clothes, electricity etc. You simply have to, or you will not survive. The good news is that there is no problem with spending on them so long as you put a limit on how much you need to spend. You see, being rich does not mean that you have to deprive yourself of the things you need. After all, you have worked hard for that money and you deserve to have a piece of it.

In spending the money you have earned, make sure that you don't go beyond the allowable limit which is 80%. Remember that the 80% should answer for all the things you need to buy or pay for. This goes to tell that you should not have expenses beyond the 80% limit. If you are earning $1200 per month, make sure that your way of living can be sustained by $960 per month and no more. This should cover your food, water and electric bills, rent (if any), transportation costs, and other expenses. If the $960 is not enough for you to last a month, you need to cut off on expenses that you don't need i.e. movie 3x/month, VIP golf membership dues, etc. In simple words, cut those expenses that would go beyond your limit.

You may ask, "Why do I need to do that when the entire $1200 can cover all that?" The answer is simple – because you want to be rich. How does spending on 80% of your income make you rich? Here's how:

- It puts a limit on spending

Since you have a ceiling on your allowable expenses, it automatically shuts off further spending on your part. The fact that you are only allowed to spend on a certain extent makes you think about not spending the rest, hence a spending limit you would not otherwise have.

- It helps you to determine which ones you really need

People often buy things they don't really need, resulting both wasted time and money. But because you are only allowed to spend 80% of your income, you are now forced to determine which ones are among the priority expenses. As such, you will have to dispense with the things you don't really need to prevent wasted resources and focus on the more important things that you need in your life.

- It allows you to have spare money

Spare money is very important in maintaining one's financial stability. Life is very uncertain and more often than not, people won't really have time to prepare for the next expenses to come. Saving 20% of your income helps you to gain some leverage financially, especially in times of need.

- It hones your skill of managing your finances

Some say that people show their ability and discipline best when confronted with boundaries or limitations. Having an 80% spending limit tests your skill in managing your finances, which in turn could hone you to become a better and wiser spender in the long run.

Now that you know what to do with 80% of your income, the next thing that you have to know is what to do with the remaining 20%. What does that 20% represent? How does that 20% make a difference in your way of life?

The remaining 20% of your income represents your savings. It is the spare money that you can count on in times of need, thus giving you some financial security and room for other necessary expenses. It gives you more power financially and more security psychologically because you won't be threatened by life events you never planned or in any way expected. In other words, you would be more economically stable. Such amount can make a huge difference between financial uncertainty and financial stability. Of course you wouldn't want to be on the bad side, would you?

However, do not be too complacent with the fact that you have saved at least 20% of your income in a storage box. The fact is, the way you manage that 20% savings is as important as the way you manage the 80% of your income. If you want to be rich, there is no question that you should manage both WISELY. But exactly how can you do that?

Here are where your savings should go:

- Business Fund

As you will learn later on, having a business investment is very important in creating wealth. Surely, you would need a capital from which you would build your business. Save a business fund for this goal as early as today so that you will have enough money when the time comes that you are ready to venture into the business world.

- Charity Fund

Set aside being filthy rich – what you need to be is a rich man with a heart. As a person, you need to help people in need whether they are complete strangers or the closest of your friends. As the law of karma always says, helping is an investment in itself. Surely, you want to reap the fruits of your good deeds later on!

- Emergency Fund

No one knows for sure what will happen next. The future is uncertain and the only way for you to be prepared for what might come is to make sure that your weapons are ready. Have an emergency fund that you can count on anytime and in any event so you won't be caught off guard!

- Car Fund

A means of transportation is also very essential in building your wealth. In order to be rich, you need to have the ability to move around places as you deal with transactions. This could only be attained by having a reliable means of transport – a car.

This car fund is not only to be used to purchase a car (if you don't have one yet); it should also be a fund ready to answer for car repairs and improvements.

- Miscellaneous Fund

Expenses which cannot be classified into a specified group should be covered under miscellaneous fund. This is where you should get the money to finance unexpected, little costs you haven't expected in your budget. This gives you a little leeway for spending on things that you need but failed to account for in your budget.

- Pleasure Fund

Truth be told, pleasure is a basic human need. Whether it is as grand as having a world cruise or a simple movie per week agenda, your pleasure has to be incorporated in your life.

All people have their own choices when it comes to what gives them pleasure, some more costly than others. The reason why you need to have a fund to answer for your pleasure expenses is so that you will never have to choose or compromise between necessities and pleasure. You can have both and still be rich! You might think that these funds cannot be covered by the 20% fund alone, and you're correct about that to an extent. But the thing is, these are some of the funds that you can utilize in times of need.

The manner on which you want to distribute the savings is up to you; you may divide the 20% equally or depending on your priorities. If you badly want a car, you may allot more to your car fund that in any other funds. You see, there is no hard and fast rule when it comes to your savings so long as you have these important fund classifications with you. All of these accounts are important for you to attain the financial stability you're aiming for.

To better utilize these funds, you can go to a reliable credit union where you can set up 6 accounts representing each fund. Aside from having them take care of your accounts of you, you can also be sure that you won't be able to spend your money on impulse as when you have the money on hand.

If you don't find (or want) a credit union to handle your savings, you can definitely just use an envelope to separate these funds under one account. Either way, you accomplish your goal of savings utilization by putting up different funds.

Thanks For Previewing My Exiting Book Entitled:

"How To Be Rich: Discover How To Be Rich Using Money Rules Of The Rich To Make Money, Gain Passive Income, Be Debt Free, And Financially Free In 6 Simple Steps!"

To purchase this book, simply go to the Amazon Kindle store and simply search:

"HOW TO BE RICH"

Then just scroll down until you see my book. You will know it is mine because you will see my name "James Harper" underneath the title.

Alternatively, you can visit my author page on Amazon to see this book and other work I have done. Thanks so much, and please don't forget your free bonuses

DON'T LEAVE YET! - CHECK OUT YOUR FREE BONUSES BELOW!

Free Bonus Offer 1: Get Free Access To The OperationAwesomeLife.com VIP Newsletter!

Free Bonus Offer 2: Get A Free Download Of My Friends Amazing Book "Passive Income" First Chapter!

Free Bonus Offer 3: Get A Free Email Series On Making Money Online When You Join Newsletter!

GET ALL 3 FREE - CLICK HERE

Once you enter your email address you will immediately get free access to this awesome **VIP NEWSLETTER!**

For a limited time, if you join for free right now, you will also get free access to the first chapter of the awesome book "**PASSIVE INCOME**"!

And, last but definitely not least, if you join the newsletter right now, you also will get a free 10 part email series on **10 SUCCESS SECRETS OF MAKING MONEY ONLINE!**

To claim all 3 of your FREE BONUSES just click below!

Just click here for all 3 VIP bonuses!

Operation Awesome Life Bonuses